Glaciers

DISCOVER PICTURES AND FACTS ABOUT GLACIERS FOR KIDS! A CHILDREN'S EARTH SCIENCES BOOK

We've probably seen pictures of glaciers, but here are some cool facts about glaciers that you should know about.

About a tenth of land is covered in some sort of glacial ice, and that includes ice caps, sheets, and glaciers.

They actually hold about 2/3 of the earth's water

During the 14th to the mid-19th century, there was actually a mini ice age, which kept temperatures cool enough for glaciers to advance around

Most glaciers are located in Alaska, and if glaciers melted, it would make the sea levels rise about 230 feet worldwide

The ice crystals within glaciers themselves can be as large as baseballs

The largest glacier in the world is the Lamber glacier, which is located in Antartica

Glacial ice flows from high to low, and it actually takes a chunk of rock with it inside of it.

The one ingredient that is needed for glaciers to form is where snow is around all the time, and when new layers arrive it crushes the existing ones

Alaskans are allowed to harvest glacial ice, provided they have a permit in order to do so.

The Antartic continent is actually at least partially covered by this all the time, and it has been for millions of years.

Glaciers are pretty, and here you learned a little bit about them.

Ingram Content Group UK Ltd.
Milton Keynes UK
UKHW051958060423
419722UK00009B/88

9 781071 708422